Masai Giraffe

African Leopard

Grevy's Zebra

Thomson's Gazelle

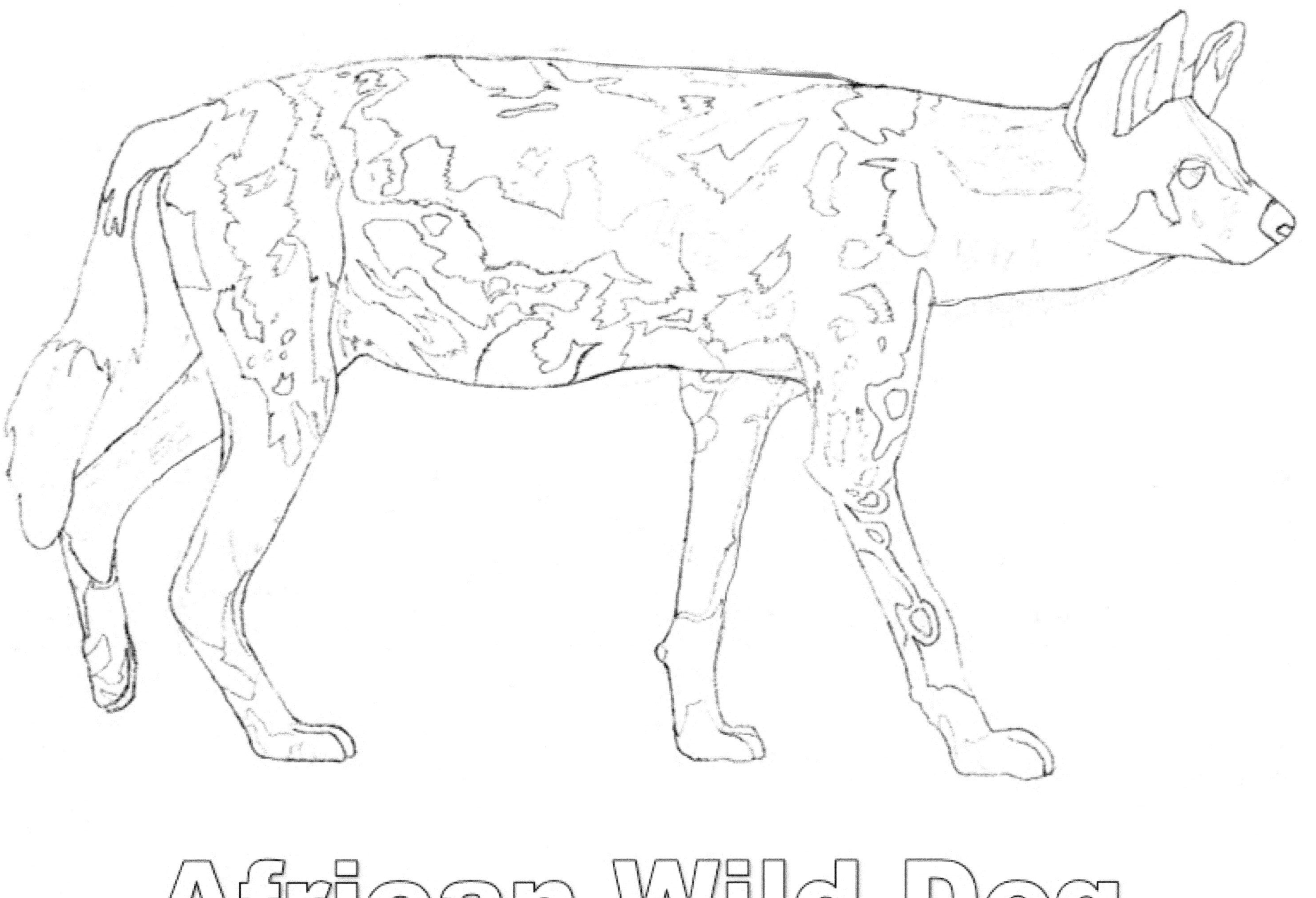

African Wild Dog

Secretary Bird

White Rhinoceros

Warthog

Ostrich

Olive Baboon

Serval

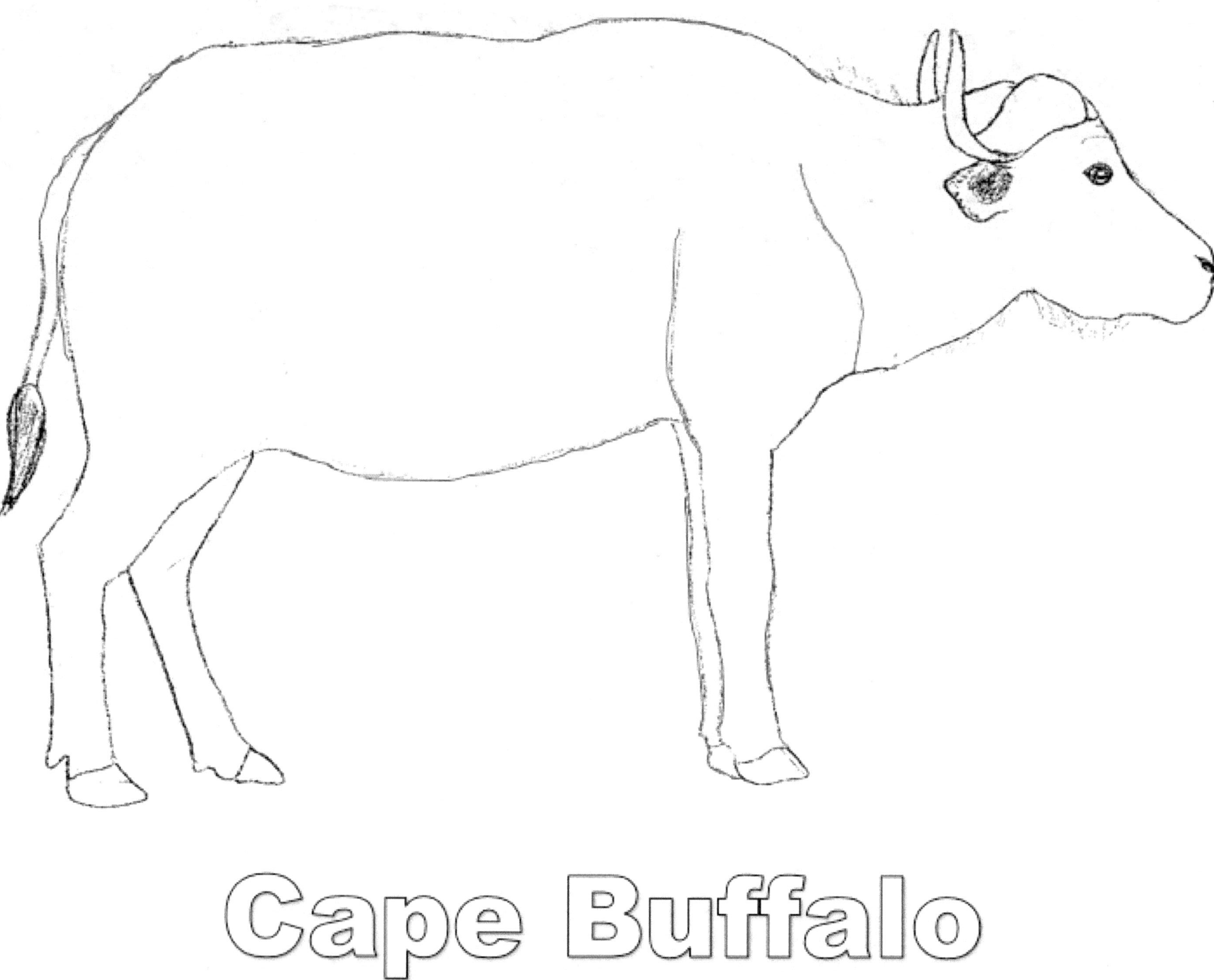

Cape Buffalo

White-Backed Vulture

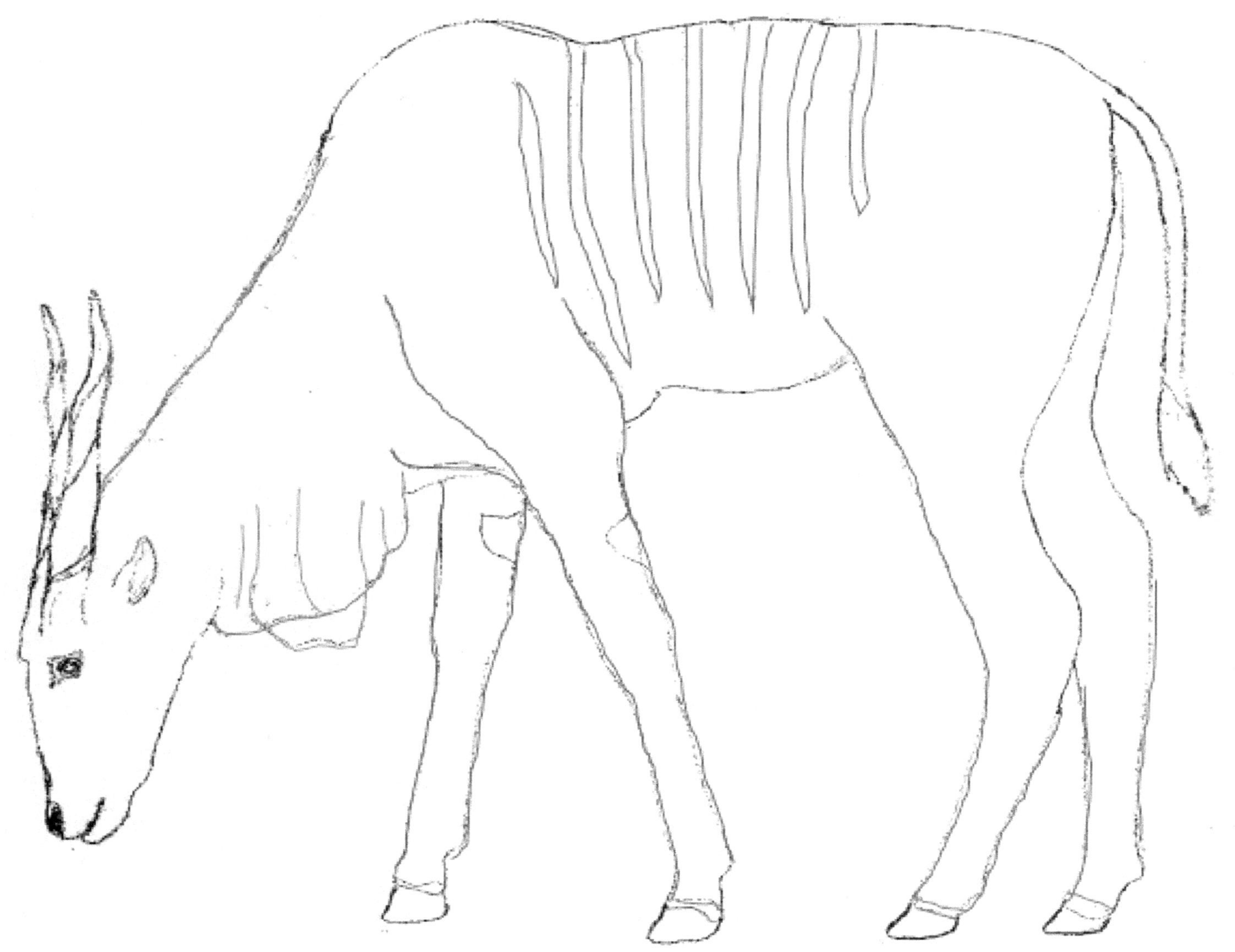

Common Eland

Aardvark

Gemsbok

Bat-Eared Fox

African Crowned Crane

African Lion

African Elephant

Wildebeest

Common Hippopotamus

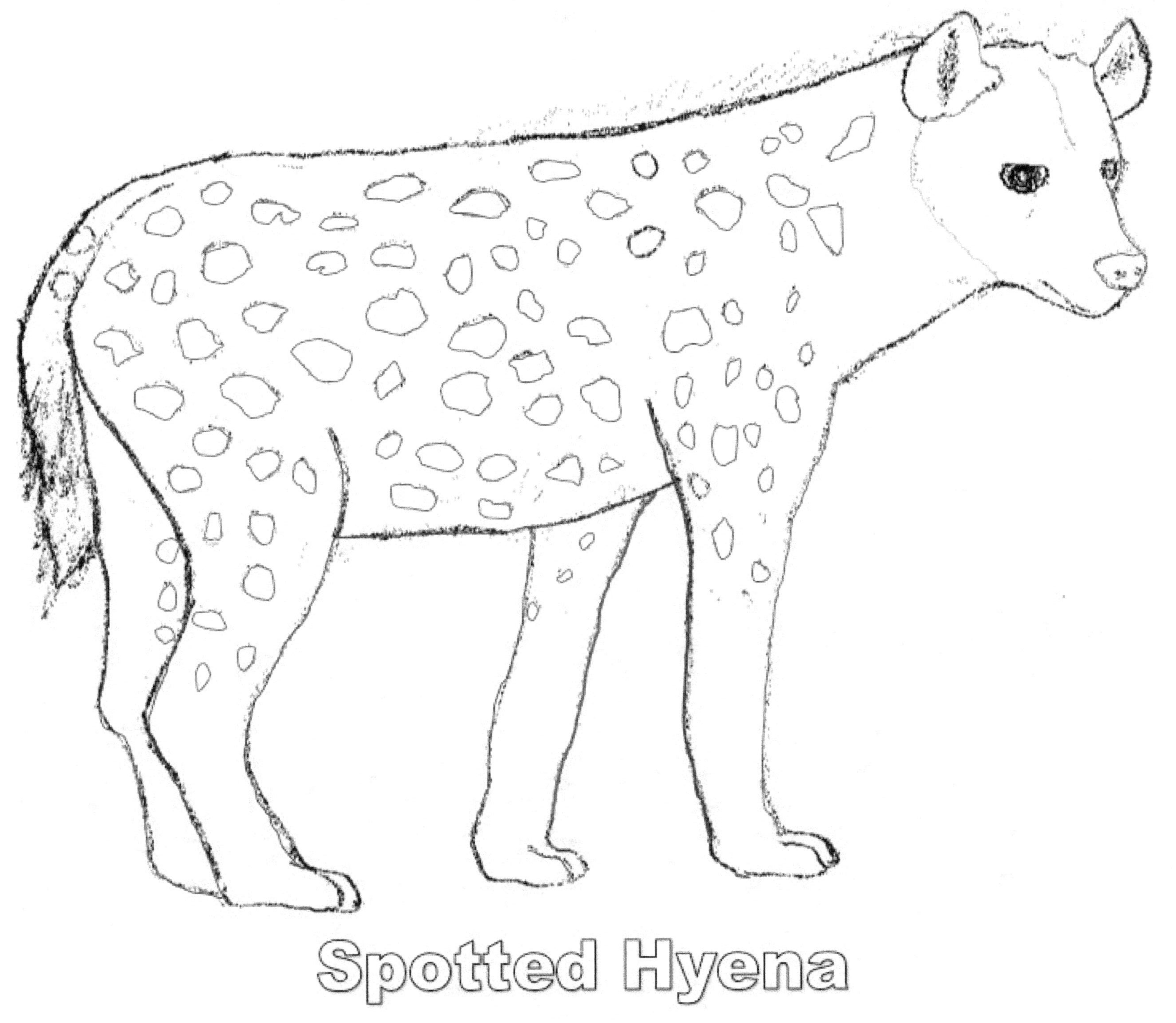

Spotted Hyena

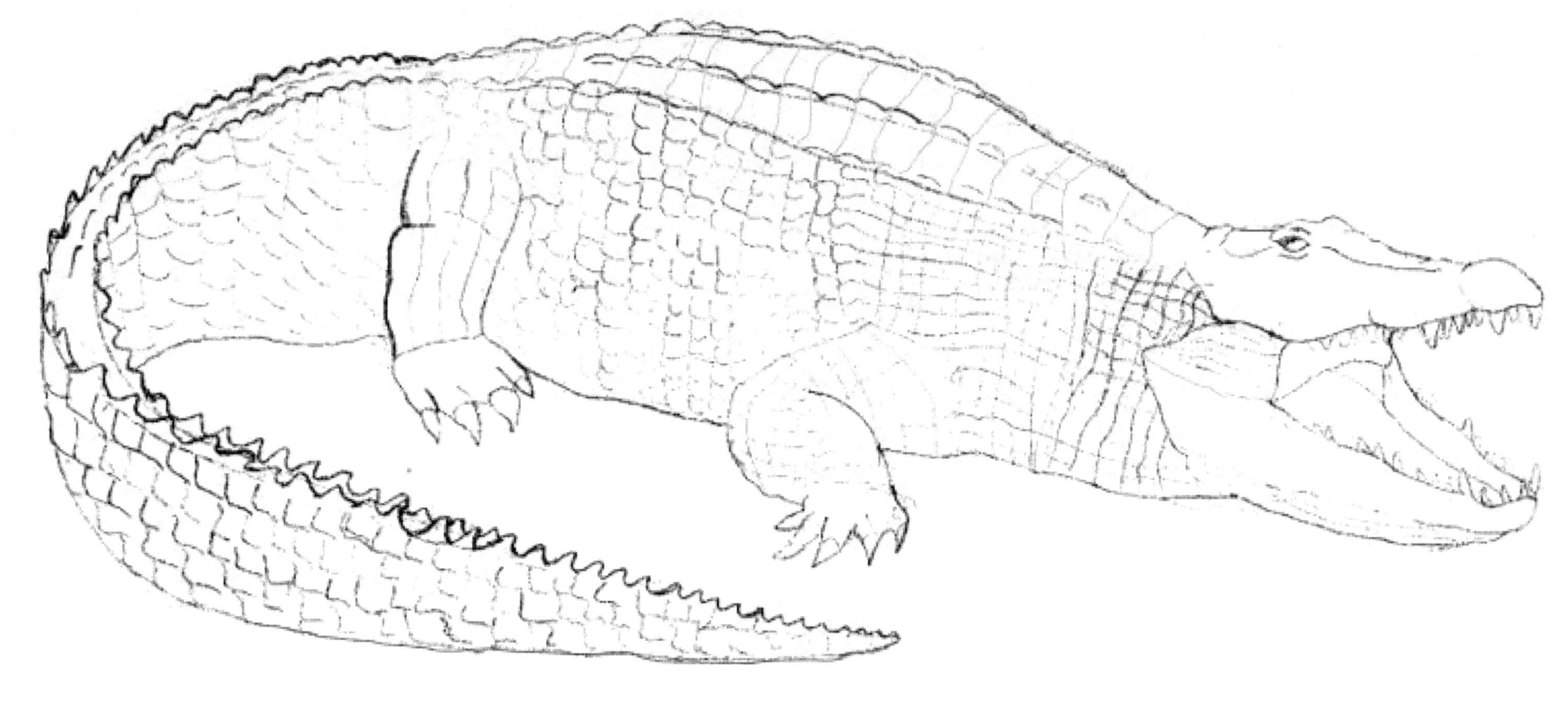

Nile Crocodile

Blue Crane

Vervet Monkey

Greater Kudu

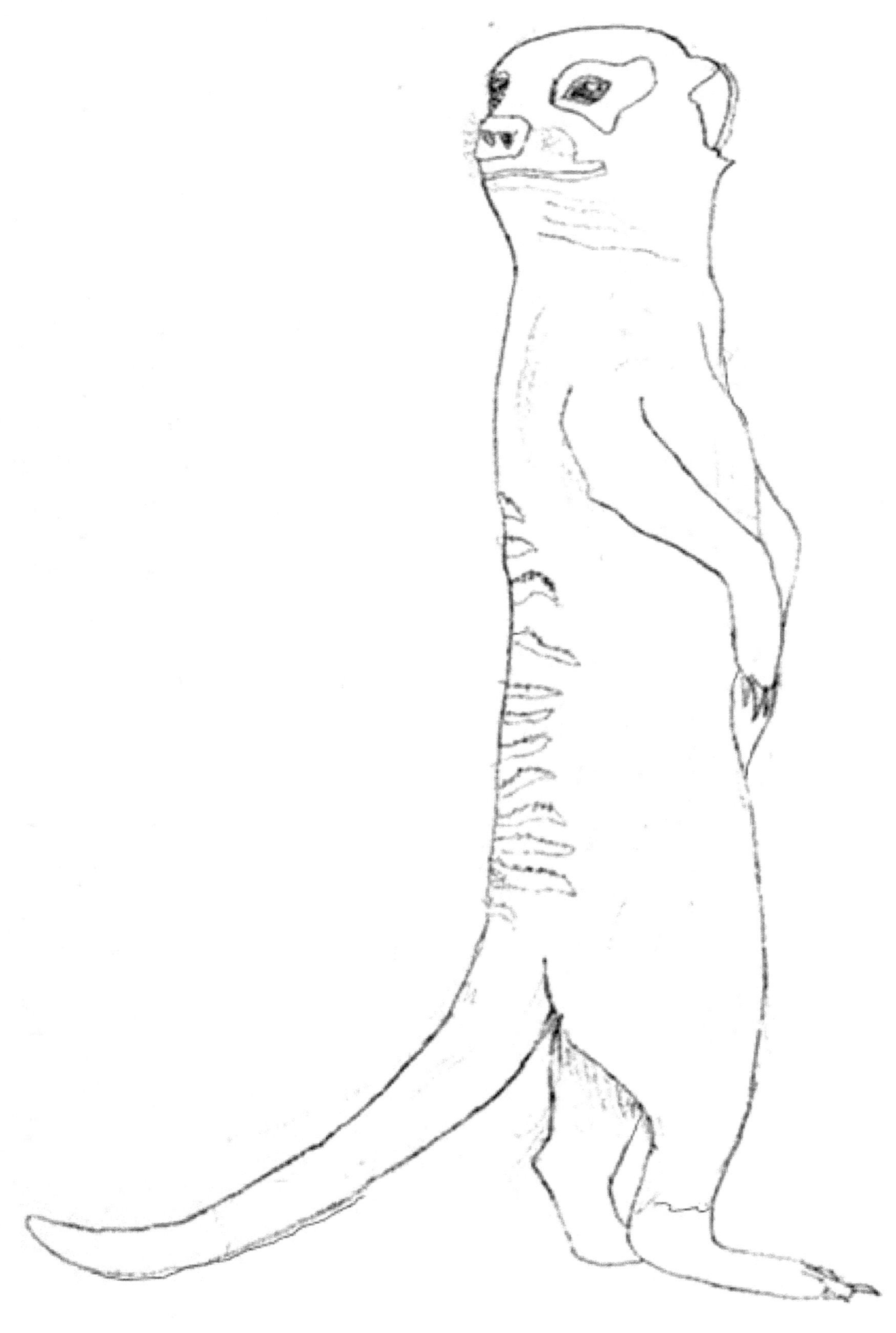

Meerkat

Impala

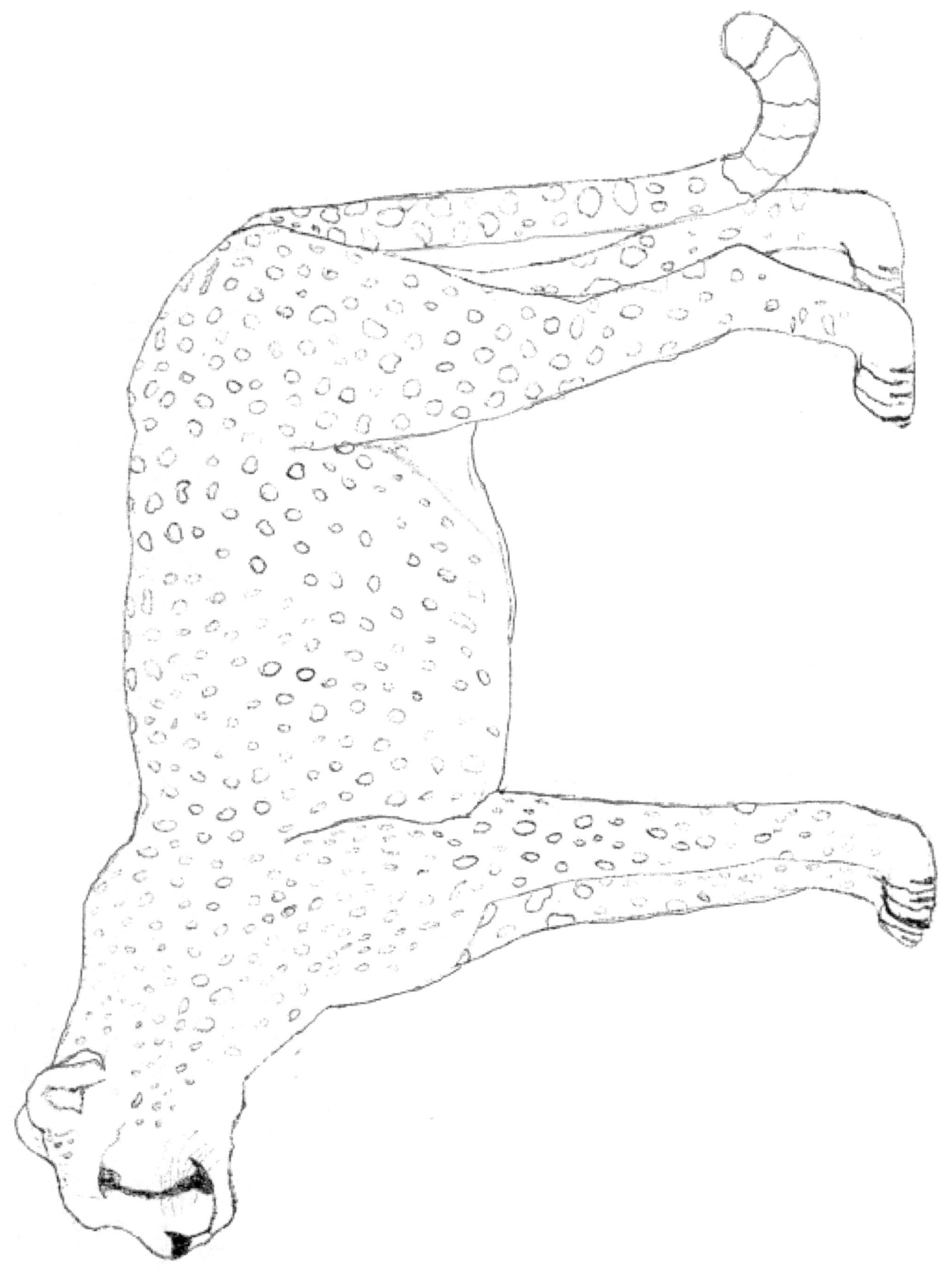

Cheetah